PIANO - VOCAL - GUITAR

ISBN 978-1-4234-8468-4

HAL•LEONARD®
CORPORATION
7777 W. BLUEMOUND RD. P.O. BOX 13819 MILWAUKEE, WI 53213

Visit Hal Leonard Online at
www.halleonard.com

WORLD WAR III

Words and Music by
NICHOLAS JONAS

PARANOID

Words and Music by NICHOLAS JONAS,
JOSEPH JONAS, KEVIN JONAS II,
CATHY DENNIS and JOHN FIELDS

FLY WITH ME

Words and Music by NICHOLAS JONAS,
JOSEPH JONAS, KEVIN JONAS II
and GREG GARBOWSKY

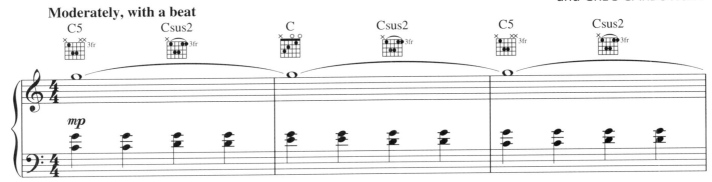

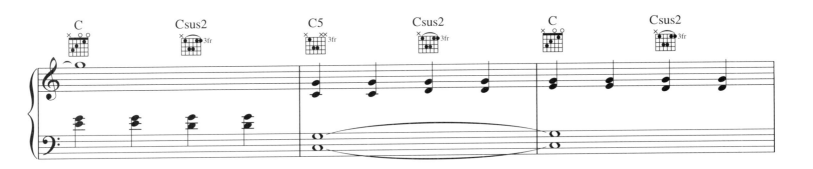

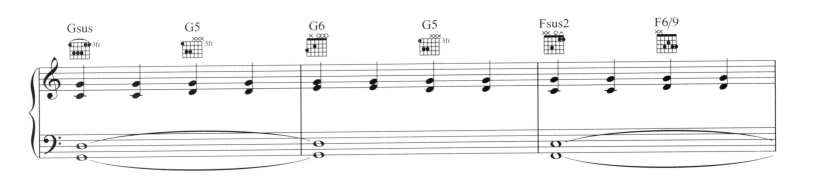

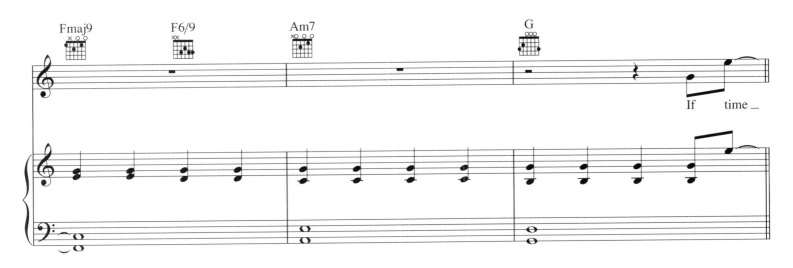

If   time ___

POISON IVY

Words and Music by NICHOLAS JONAS,
JOSEPH JONAS, KEVIN JONAS II
and GREG GARBOWSKY

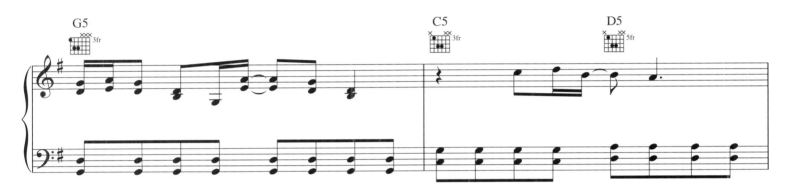

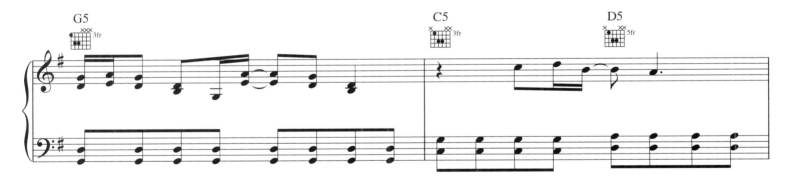

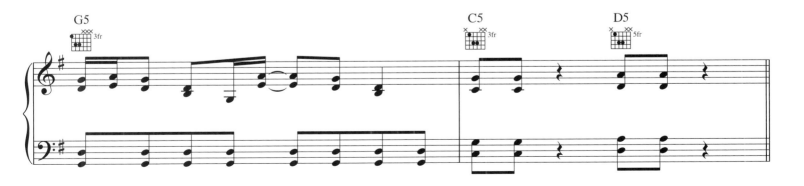

HEY BABY

Words and Music by NICHOLAS JONAS,
JOSEPH JONAS and KEVIN JONAS II

42

BEFORE THE STORM

Words and Music by NICHOLAS JONAS,
JOSEPH JONAS, KEVIN JONAS II
and MILEY CYRUS

WHAT DID I DO TO YOUR HEART

Words and Music by NICHOLAS JONAS,
JOSEPH JONAS and KEVIN JONAS II

Energetic Pop Rock

Ba - by girl I'm just a bit con - fused, you've been act - ing like you've

All I ev - er get is at - ti - tude, con - stant nev - er end - ing

MUCH BETTER

Words and Music by NICHOLAS JONAS,
JOSEPH JONAS and KEVIN JONAS II

Get a rep for break-ing hearts, ___
en - e - mies, ___

now I'm done with su - per-stars. ___
and they're all friends sud - den - ly. ___

All the tears on
B F F's e -

*Recorded a half step higher.

You're much bet - ter, girl. _____

You, _____
Lead vocal ad lib to end

you. _____

BLACK KEYS

Words and Music by NICHOLAS JONAS,
JOSEPH JONAS and KEVIN JONAS II

68

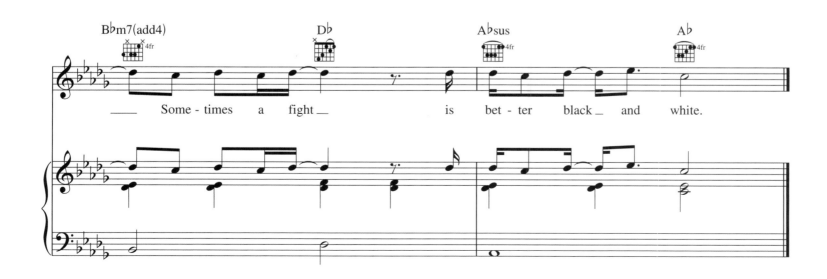

DON'T CHARGE ME
FOR THE CRIME

Words and Music by NICHOLAS JONAS,
JOSEPH JONAS, KEVIN JONAS II,
LONNIE RASHID LYNN JR. and RYAN LIESTMAN

Moderate Rock, with a groove

Spoken: *"This is life in this world. Some things go right, some things go wrong. It's just how the world can be.*

People just want to be free, yeah."

The

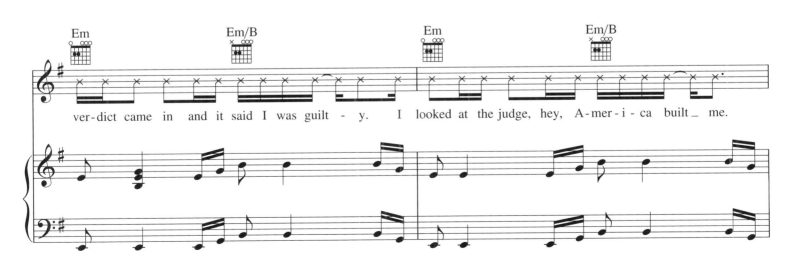

ver-dict came in and it said I was guilt - y. I looked at the judge, hey, A-mer-i-ca built _ me.

TURN RIGHT

Words and Music by NICHOLAS JONAS,
JOSEPH JONAS and KEVIN JONAS II

DON'T SPEAK

Words and Music by NICHOLAS JONAS,
JOSEPH JONAS and KEVIN JONAS II

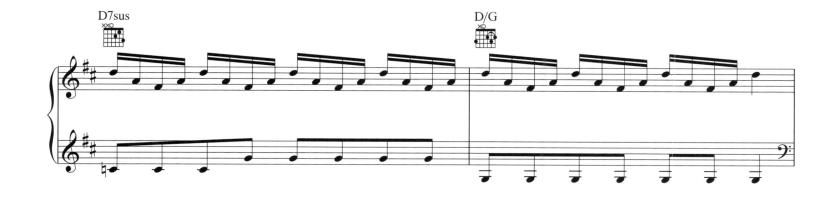

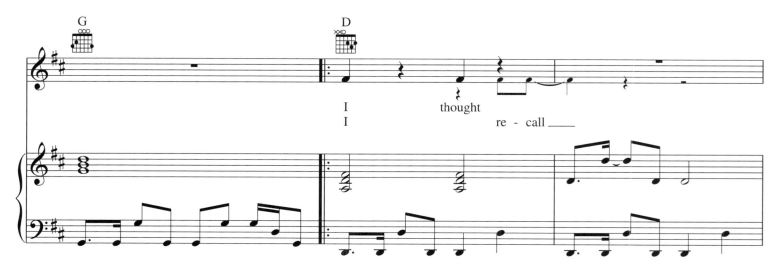

I thought

I re - call _____

F♯m
Bm
I was cool, but I just
all our fights, most of all,
C
looked a fool for so long.
all the times you would lie
G
Gm
Now you're gone,
in my arms,
Gm/A
D
now you're gone, yeah.
now you're gone. you're
3fr
3fr

KEEP IT REAL

Words and Music by NICHOLAS JONAS,
JOSEPH JONAS and KEVIN JONAS II

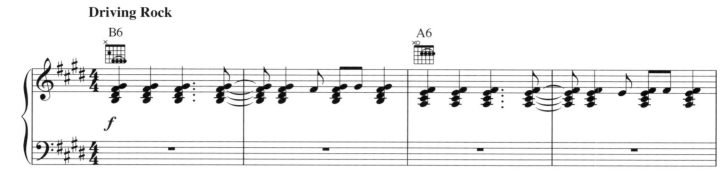

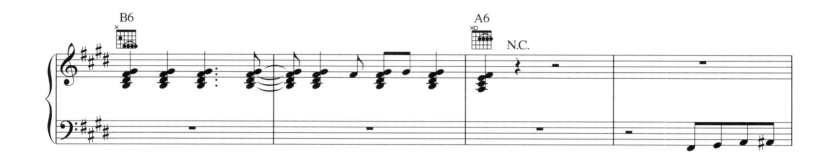

There _